Editor
Eric Migliaccio

Managing Editor
Ina Massler Levin, M.A.

Editor-in-Chief
Sharon Coan, M.S. Ed.

Illustrator
Sue Fullam

Cover Artist
Janet Chadwick

Art Manager
Kevin Barnes

Imaging
Ralph Olmedo, Jr.
Rosa C. See

Product Manager
Phil Garcia

Publishers
Rachelle Cracchiolo, M.S. Ed.
Mary Dupuy Smith, M.S. Ed.

Grammar, Usage & Mechanics

GRADE 2

Author

Melissa Hart, M.F.A.

Teacher Created Materials, Inc.
6421 Industry Way
Westminster, CA 92683
www.teachercreated.com
ISBN-0-7439-3779-1
©2003 Teacher Created Materials, Inc.
Made in U.S.A.

Table of Contents

Introduction 3

Parts of Speech

    Object Nouns 4

    People Nouns 6

    Place Nouns 8

    Action Verbs 10

    Helping Verbs 13

    Complete Sentences 16

    Adjectives 18

    Adverbs 20

Punctuation

    Capitalization 22

    Periods. 24

    Commas 25

    Periods and Commas Combined. 26

    Question Marks. 27

    Exclamation Marks. 28

    Question Marks and Exclamation Marks Combined 29

Usage

    Sentence Fragments 30

    Run-on Sentences 32

    Too Many Words. 34

Putting It All Together

    Editing a Story 36

    Telling a Story. 38

    Sharing Your Work 40

    The Finished Piece! 41

Assessment 42

Answer Key 47

Introduction

The idea that "practice makes perfect" relates directly to your child's education. The more practice your child receives in concepts that are taught in school, the more likely that he or she will excel. Many parents know the value of practicing a subject learned in school, but the lack of readily available resources can be frustrating.

As a parent, it is also difficult to know where to focus your efforts so that the practice your child receives at home supports what he or she is being taught at school.

This book was written with the goal of helping both parents and teachers reinforce basic language skills with children. *Practice Makes Perfect: Grammar, Usage, & Mechanics* reviews grammar skills for second grade students. The exercises in this book can be completed sequentially or out of order, as needed.

Completing this book will help your second grader meet the standards and objectives listed below. These are similar to those required by your state and school district for second-grade students.

- The student uses nouns and verbs in written compositions.

- The student uses adjectives and adverbs in written compositions.

- The student uses capitalization appropriately.

- The student uses periods after declarative sentences.

- The student uses question marks after interrogative sentences.

- The student uses commas in a series of words.

- The student uses strategies to organize written work.

- The student evaluates own and others' writing.

- The student uses strategies to draft and revise written work.

How to Make the Most of This Book

Here are some ideas to be used in conjunction with this book:

- Set aside a special place in your home for grammar practice. Keep the area tidy, with the book and favorite writing implements close at hand.

- Set up a particular time of day to work on practice pages. This establishes consistency.

- Help beginning readers to understand the written instructions at the top of each practice page.

- Keep all practice sessions with your child positive. If your child becomes frustrated, set the book aside for a period of time. Do not use this book as punishment.

- Review the work your child has done. Pay attention to those areas in which your child has the most difficulty. Provide extra guidance and further practice in those areas.

- Find ways to apply your child's new skills to everyday life. Play games with your child, and read everything—from the back of cereal boxes to comics—in order to reinforce skills.

Object Nouns

A *noun* is a person, place, or object. Here are some examples of nouns that are objects: **cat**, **dirt**, **apple**, **book**, **sky**.

Study how these nouns are used in a sentence.

⇨ The **cat** ran up the tree.

⇨ She planted corn in the **dirt**.

⇨ I eat an **apple** each day.

⇨ Open your math **book**.

⇨ The **sky** is full of stars.

Write down five object nouns of your own in the box below.

Now, write five sentences, using all five of your nouns.

1. _____

2. _____

3. _____

4. _____

5. _____

Object Nouns *(cont.)*

Fill in the blank spaces with nouns that are objects. The first one has been done for you.

1. Today, I found a lost _____ dog _____ .

2. The _____ cried in her crib.

3. My pet _____ swam in its bowl.

4. For dinner, we'll eat _____ .

5. I like to ride my _____ .

6. Dad swept the floor with a _____ .

7. Put on your _____ . It's cold outside.

8. Eek! I saw a _____ .

People Nouns

Nouns can also be people. Here are some examples: **Mom**, **babysitter**, **Mrs. Smith**, **nurse**, **man**.

Study how these nouns are used in a sentence.

⇨ I cooked breakfast for **Mom**.

⇨ My **babysitter** dances with me.

⇨ We brought **Mrs. Smith** her mail.

⇨ The **nurse** took his temperature.

⇨ The elderly **man** likes to sing.

Write down five people nouns of your own in the box below.

Now, write five sentences, using all five of your nouns.

1. _____

2. _____

3. _____

4. _____

5. _____

People Nouns *(cont.)*

Fill in the blank spaces with nouns that are people. The first one has been done for you.

1. My _____**brother**_____ has a new bike.

2. The _____ wrote on the chalkboard.

3. _____ got a new parrot.

4. "Clean up your room," said _____ .

5. The _____ at the library gave me a book.

6. _____ drove the car too fast.

7. _____ likes to juggle and tell jokes.

8. Your _____ takes good care of you.

Place Nouns

Finally, nouns can be places. Here are some examples: **California**, **Atlantic Ocean**, **Mexico**, **classroom**, **Mars**.

Study how these nouns are used in a sentence.

⇨ We live in **California**.

⇨ Pilgrims sailed across the **Atlantic Ocean**.

⇨ **Mexico** has pretty beaches.

⇨ She loves to sit in the **classroom**.

⇨ When I grow up, I want to go to **Mars**.

Write down five place nouns of your own in the box below.

Now, write five sentences, using all five of your nouns.

1. _____

2. _____

3. _____

4. _____

5. _____

Place Nouns *(cont.)*

Fill in the blank spaces with nouns that are places. The first one has been done for you.

1. _____ Florida _____ has many alligators.

2. I sing in the choir at _____ .

3. We shop at the _____ .

4. I live in the state of _____ .

5. The White House is in _____ .

6. I like to watch clowns at the _____ .

7. _____ is the planet on which we live.

8. My country is called _____ .

Action Verbs

An *action verb* tells what someone or something does. Here are some examples of action verbs: **run**, **jumped**, **cry**, **fell**, **dances**.

Study how these action verbs are used in a sentence.

⇨ I **run** to the school bus.

⇨ Joe **jumped** out of the tree.

⇨ We **cry** if we get hurt.

⇨ She **fell** off her bike.

⇨ My brother **dances** with the dog.

Write down five action verbs of your own in the box below.

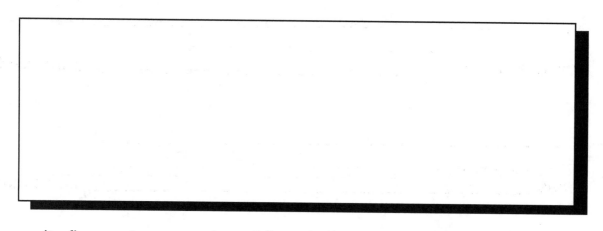

Now, write five sentences, using all five of your action verbs.

1. _____

2. _____

3. _____

4. _____

5. _____

Action Verbs *(cont.)*

Fill in the blank spaces with action verbs. The first one has been done for you.

1. The cat __licked__ its fur.

2. Grandma _____ through the park.

3. The leaves _____ in the wind.

4. Jonas _____ in the mud.

5. Her dad _____ the car.

6. The teacher _____ the pencil.

7. The baby _____ the milk.

More Action Verbs

Circle the action verbs in the sentences below and write them on the line.

1. Mom cooked spaghetti.

2. The bread baked in the oven.

3. We ate as much as we could.

4. Jan played her guitar.

5. We clapped our hands.

6. Everyone sang songs.

7. Dad and I washed dishes.

8. We eat spaghetti a lot.

Helping Verbs

Helping verbs are verbs that do not show action. Here are some examples of helping verbs: **is**, **were**, **feel**, **looks**, **seemed**.

Study how these helping verbs are used in a sentence.

⇨ Tomas **is** a lucky boy.

⇨ There **were** two squirrels in our yard.

⇨ I **feel** sick today.

⇨ Mary **looks** taller than her sister.

⇨ Dad **seemed** happy with his new tie.

Write down five helping verbs of your own in the box below.

Now, write five sentences, using all five of your helping verbs.

1. _____

2. _____

3. _____

4. _____

5. _____

Helping Verbs *(cont.)*

Fill in the blank spaces with helping verbs. The first one has been done for you.

1. We _____ were _____ so tired.

2. I _____ cold.

3. You _____ mad.

4. Yesterday, Mr. Cross _____ happy.

5. That soup _____ delicious.

6. _____ you ready to go?

7. The wet, muddy kitten _____ lost.

8. Greg _____ glad to go home.

More Helping Verbs

Circle the helping verbs in the sentences below and write them on the line.

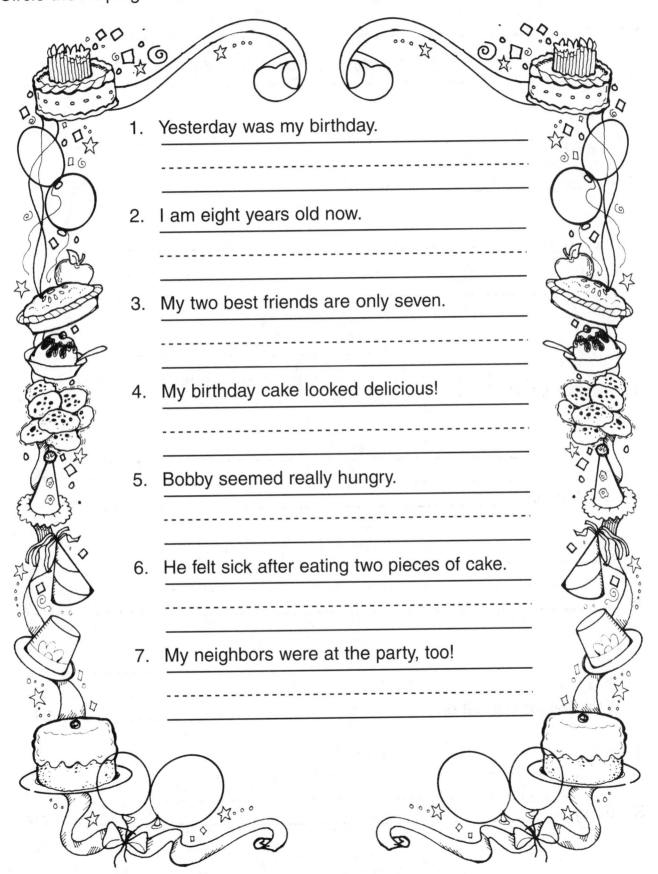

1. Yesterday was my birthday.

2. I am eight years old now.

3. My two best friends are only seven.

4. My birthday cake looked delicious!

5. Bobby seemed really hungry.

6. He felt sick after eating two pieces of cake.

7. My neighbors were at the party, too!

Complete Sentences

A *complete sentence* has both a *subject* and a *predicate*. A subject tells who or what the sentence is about. A predicate tells what the subject is or does. (*Hint:* The predicate contains the verb.)

Here are some examples of complete sentences. The subject is circled, and the predicate is underlined.

⇨ (The elephant) <u>likes to eat hay.</u>
   subject   predicate

⇨ (Father) <u>made a birthday cake.</u>
   subject   predicate

⇨ (That tractor) <u>is so noisy!</u>
   subject   predicate

⇨ (Mrs. Diaz) <u>sewed a quilt.</u>
   subject   predicate

⇨ (The bird) <u>is feeding her babies.</u>
   subject   predicate

Now, read the sentences below. Circle the subject and underline the predicate in each sentence.

1. Jim and John play kickball on the field.

2. The computer is making funny noises.

3. Katie's hamster loves carrots.

4. The crow stole the farmer's corn.

5. You like to ride your bike in the rain.

Complete Sentences (cont.)

Finish the following sentences with a **predicate** to make them complete.

1. Bobby _____ .

2. The police officer _____ .

3. The alarm clock _____ .

4. Grandfather _____ .

5. The North Pole _____ .

Now, begin the following sentences with a **subject** to make them complete.

6. _____ kicked the ball onto the roof.

7. _____ drinks milk out of a bowl.

8. _____ rang, scaring my mother.

9. _____ gave me a birthday present.

10. _____ howled when it heard the siren.

Adjectives

An *adjective* describes a noun. Here are some examples of adjectives: **pretty, blue, fast, loud, silly**.

Study how these adjectives are used in a sentence.

⇨ The **pretty** baby clapped her hands.

⇨ Their toy wagon is **blue**.

⇨ Mike likes his **fast** car.

⇨ She played **loud** music all night.

⇨ Those **silly** boys laugh all the time.

Study the sentences below. Underline the adjective in each sentence, and circle the noun it describes.

1. The yellow daisies glow in the sun.

2. He lifted the heavy box.

3. That tree has red leaves.

4. Aunt Ginny is tall.

5. The moon was big and bright as it shone last night.

Adjectives *(cont.)*

Fill in the blank spaces with adjectives to describe the nouns. The first one has been done for you.

1. That _____ big _____ bear stole our lunch.

2. My sister's hair is _____ .

3. The _____ monkey ate a peanut.

4. Mrs. Mumbles found a _____ dollar.

5. I had a _____ piece of cake in my lunch bag.

6. Recess was _____ today.

7. I am a _____ , _____ child.

8. My house is _____ and _____ .

Adverbs

Adverbs are words that describe verbs, adjectives, or other adverbs. Here are some examples of adverbs: **slowly**, **joyfully**, **carefully**, **sadly**, **quietly**.

Study how these adverbs are used in a sentence.

⇨ The snake slid **slowly** through the grass.

⇨ The bride and groom danced **joyfully**.

⇨ Mrs. Davis **carefully** washed the cat.

⇨ **Sadly**, we swept up the broken glass.

⇨ I walked **quietly** down the stairs.

Study the sentences below. Underline the adverb in each sentence, and circle the word it describes.

1. The photographer quickly snapped a picture.

2. Martha sings beautifully.

3. The doctor spoke gently to the patient.

4. The leaves shook crazily in the storm.

5. My brother and I warmly shook hands.

Adverbs *(cont.)*

Fill in the blank spaces with adverbs. Next, circle the word that the adverb describes. The first one has been done for you.

1. She _____ slowly _____ (rode) her bicycle home.

2. They walked _____ down the dusty mountain road.

3. My goldfish swims _____ in its bowl.

4. He runs _____ fast.

5. Misty wrote _____ on the test.

6. The man talked _____ , and I couldn't understand him.

7. The ice cracked _____ under my feet.

8. If you dress _____ , you can go.

Capitalization

There are a few rules to follow when it comes to *capitalization*.

⇨ Always capitalize the first word of a sentence.
Example: **L**ions live in Africa.

⇨ Capitalize a person's name.
Example: **C**athy **C**arter likes to juggle.

⇨ Capitalize titles before a person's name.
Example: **D**r. Lee loves children.

⇨ Capitalize the names of streets, cities, states, and countries.
Example: I live on **M**ain **S**treet in **P**ortland, **O**regon.

Study the sentences below. Circle the letters that need to be capitalized. Then, rewrite the sentence correctly.

1. last week, julie broke her leg.

   _____

   -

   _____

2. mr. harris lives in Kentucky.

   _____

   -

   _____

3. do you like to watch bugs bunny on T.V.?

   _____

   -

   _____

4. Suzie told mom she wanted to go to canada.

   _____

   -

   _____

5. dr. roberts lives in the united states.

   _____

   -

   _____

Capitalization (cont.)

Read each noun in the boxes below. Color the boxes with words that need to be capitalized blue. Color the boxes with words that don't need to be capitalized red.

mrs. marie	truck	ohio
uncle joseph	apple	dr. ruiz
cup	city	aunt cynthia
england	teacher	bird

Periods

Use a period at the end of a sentence.

Examples:

⇨ My teacher is nice**.**

⇨ Please close the window**.**

Use a period after most abbreviations.

Examples:

⇨ Mr**.** Yang likes to surf.

⇨ Dr**.** Bates wants a pet rat.

Rewrite the following sentences. Add periods where they are needed.

1. Ms Bee ran for the bus

   _____

   -

   _____

2. The snake bit Dr John on his toe

   _____

   -

   _____

3. I like to eat ice cream

   _____

   -

   _____

4. Both Jose Jr and Mr Sam love boats

   _____

   -

   _____

5. Ask Dr Brown if you can have a lollipop

   _____

   -

   _____

Commas

Use a comma after the greeting of a letter.

Examples:

⇨ Dear George, How are you?

⇨ Dear Sara, Will you marry me?

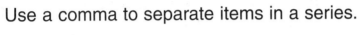

Use a comma to separate items in a series.

Examples:

⇨ Dad bought eggs, milk, and bread at the store.

⇨ You will see the monkey, the tiger, and the snake at the zoo.

Rewrite the following sentences. Add commas where they are needed.

1. Dear Cathy Thank you for the gift.

   _____

2. We like to run hike and ski.

   _____

3. Dear Sam I like you.

   _____

4. Do you want milk juice or water?

   _____

5. My friends are named Charlie Liz and Kitty.

   _____

Periods and Commas Combined

Add periods and commas to the following sentences, where needed:

1. Mrs Jones walked a mile

2. She went to the library the store and the park

3. Dr Katt fed ducks at the park

4. Children threw bread crackers and cookies for the ducks

5. Ralph John and Jenny played on the swings.

6. Mr Jones brought his wife a letter

7. It said, "Dear Mrs Jones Please call me."

8. You left your book at the store

Question Marks

Use a question mark after you ask a question.

Examples:

⇨ Are you in second grade**?**   ⇨ Where is your mother**?**

Read the following sentences. Add question marks where they are needed.

1. Who likes chocolate cake

2. How do you ride a bike

3. What is your favorite color

4. Why is the sky blue

5. When will I get a puppy

Exclamation Marks

Use an exclamation mark after you make an exclamation.

Examples:

⇨ Ouch! The snake bit me.   ⇨ Watch out for that car!

Read the following sentences. Add exclamation marks where they are needed.

1. Wow This is a fun party.

2. Hurry up and clean your room

3. I am so angry

4. Look out for the shark

5. Help Call the police

Question Marks and Exclamation Marks Combined

Add question marks or exclamation marks to the following sentences, where needed. If you're not sure which mark to add, read the sentence out loud.

1. Are you afraid of spiders _____

2. I am so scared _____

3. Who likes insects _____

4. Where can you find worms _____

5. Hurry and run from that bee _____

6. Which bug is your favorite _____

7. Watch out for the hornet _____

8. How do you catch a firefly _____

Sentence Fragments

Sentence fragments occur when a sentence is missing either a noun or a verb.

Example: going to the doctor's office.

Correction: Dennis is going to the doctor's office.

Example: My friend Robin

Correction: My friend Robin skated across the pond.

Study the sentence fragments below. Add either a subject or a verb to correct the fragments. Don't forget to add punctuation to your new sentence.

1. Timmy Jones

2. paints happy faces

3. the airplane pilot

4. likes to watch movies

5. the house on the corner

Sentence Fragments *(cont.)*

Look at the subjects below. Look at the predicates. Match each subject with a predicate to make a complete sentence. Write the sentences in the spaces below. Don't forget to capitalize the first letter of each sentence and add a period at the end of each sentence.

Subjects

Aunt Mary
the baby rabbit
that old car
my dad
the cafeteria

Predicates

got a flat tire
smells like cookies
eats lettuce
likes soap operas
wears purple neckties

Complete Sentences

1. _____

2. _____

3. _____

4. _____

5. _____

Run-On Sentences

Run-on sentences occur when sentences are missing a period between them.

    Example: She walked he ran to the park

    Correction: She walked. He ran to the park.

Run-on sentences also occur when a word is missing from a sentence.

    Example: I love dogs cats love me.

    Correction: I love dogs, but cats love me.

Study the run-on sentences below. Rewrite them, correcting them with periods and capital letters.

1. Deanne drank milk her sister drank soda.

2. The horse ran then he jumped over the stream.

3. Peter loves cookies he eats them all day.

4. I lost my lunchbox I lost my pencil, too.

5. Ducks quack cows moo.

Run-On Sentences *(cont.)*

Rewrite the following sentences. Correct any run-ons.

1. The girls played soccer they love that game.

2. Cynthia wants shoes for her birthday She wants shorts, too.

3. The girls watch soccer on television They cheer loudly.

4. Kick the ball Now, run!

5. The field is damp the girls slide on the grass.

6. They went out for pizza They also had a slumber party.

Too Many Words

Sometimes writers add too many words to their sentences. It makes sentences difficult to read.

Example: I am telling you the honest truth.

Correction: I am telling you the truth.

Explanation: The truth is already honest.

Example: He gave his mother a big, huge gold watch.

Correction: He gave his mother a big gold watch.

Explanation: "Big" and "huge" mean the same thing.

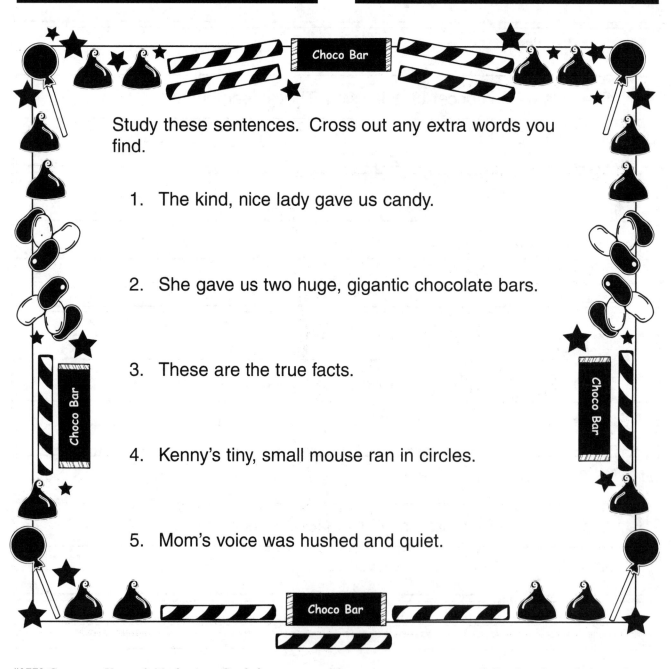

Study these sentences. Cross out any extra words you find.

1. The kind, nice lady gave us candy.

2. She gave us two huge, gigantic chocolate bars.

3. These are the true facts.

4. Kenny's tiny, small mouse ran in circles.

5. Mom's voice was hushed and quiet.

Too Many Words (cont.)

The story below contains too many words. Read it out loud, and cross out any extra words you find.

John was short in size. He wanted to be a giant, tall boy. He hung upside down from a tree. That was a failure that didn't work. He walked on his toes. His feet hurt and ached. Finally, John yelled and shouted for his brothers. Paul pulled his legs. Kevin pulled his head. John yelled, "Stop and halt!" His face was red in color. He decided he liked and enjoyed being short, after all.

Editing a Story

When you correct a story, you edit it. It is important that you have a simple way of marking a paper so everyone knows what to correct. Read the chart below. It shows you how to mark errors in a story.

Add a period.	⊙	The bat flew into the cave⊙
Add a comma.	⌃	He ate carrots⌃apples, and crackers.
Capitalize the letter.	≡	S̲sam is nine today.
Spell the word correctly.	sp	^{sp}Jumf as high as you can.　　Jump
Use a lowercase letter.	/	Today is his /Birthday!　　birthday
Begin a new paragraph.	¶	I have a dog for a pet. His name is ¶ Duke. He is brown and has big eyes. I also have a cat. Her name is Daisy. She is orange and has sharp claws.

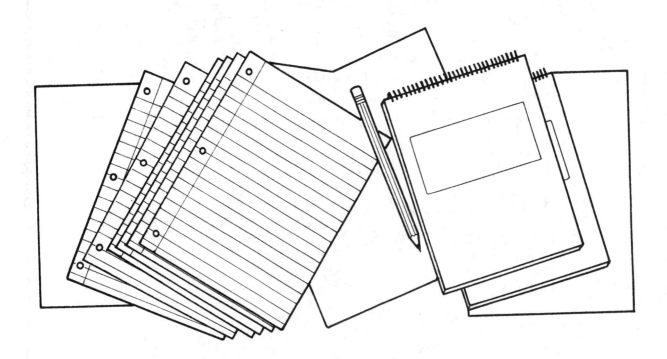

Editing a Story (cont.)

Read the story below. It has lots of errors, and it is your job to correct it. Use the editing marks you have just learned.

Here is a checklist of the types of errors you will be looking for when you read this story.

☐ Periods ⊙

☐ Commas ⌄

☐ Capitals ≡

☐ Spelling SP

☐ Lowercase letters /

☐ Appropriate paragraphs ¶

Dolphins and Chimpanzees

My favorite Animals are dolphins They are very smart.

Some peeple think dolphins are fish, but they are wrong!

Dolphins are mammals. I also like chimpanzees. They are

smart, too. If I had a pet chimpanzee, I would name him

cecil. Do you know what chimpanzees eat? They like to

eat plants meat and insects I don't know if I'd want Cecil

eeting insects!

Telling a Story

A story has several pieces. Here are the most important:

⇨ **people and/or animals.**
   Examples: Cindy Lou, a dog named Skip, Steve and Bob

⇨ **a place**
   Examples: my backyard, the ocean, a graveyard

⇨ **a time**
   Examples: midnight, 1950, the future

⇨ **a plot**
   Examples: a bad report card, a trip to Disneyland, a broken arm

⇨ **a beginning, a middle, and an end.**

Fill in the blanks to finish the story below.

The Cat in the Tree

Jamie owned a cat named _____ *(character)*. She lived in _____ *(place)*,

where there were tall trees. One _____ *(time)* the cat ran up a tree.

"Help!" cried Jamie. She shook a bag of cat food. The _____ *(animal)*

would not come down. Her _____ *(person)* called "Here, kitty!"

The cat still wouldn't come down. Finally, Jamie's brother brought out a cage.

Inside the cage was a pet mouse. He set the cage on the _____ *(place)*.

Suddenly, the cat ran down the tree. Jamie was so happy!

Telling a Story *(cont.)*

Now, write your own story in the space below. If you need help, look at the previous page for ideas.

_____

- -

_____

- -

_____

- -

_____

- -

_____

- -

_____

- -

_____

- -

_____

Use this checklist again to check your work.

☐ Periods	⊙	☐ Spelling	SP
☐ Commas	⌄	☐ Lowercase letters	/
☐ Capitals	═	☐ Appropriate paragraphs	¶

Sharing Your Work

Many writers like to share their stories with someone else before they rewrite them. This makes the stories better.

Have your friend, parent, or teacher read your story. Now, have the person you chose answer the following question below.

What questions do you have about this story?

_____

_____

_____

_____

_____

_____

_____

In the space below, write one or two more sentences for your story, to answer your partner's question.

_____

_____

_____

_____

_____

_____

_____

_____

The Finished Piece!

Now, write your finished story on the lines below.

Assessment

Fill in the bubbles in front of the correct answer for each group of choices.

1. **Mr. Myers bought a red car**
   - ⓐ Mr Myers bought a red car
   - ⓑ Mr Myers bought a red car.
   - ⓒ Mr. Myers bought a red car.
   - ⓓ No mistakes.

2. **jody lives in Alaska.**
   - ⓐ Jody lives in alaska.
   - ⓑ Jody lives in Alaska.
   - ⓒ jody lives in Alaska.
   - ⓓ No mistakes.

3. **Mom bought apples, oranges, and pears.**
   - ⓐ Mom bought apples oranges, and pears.
   - ⓑ Mom bought, apples, oranges, and pears.
   - ⓒ Mom bought apples oranges and pears.
   - ⓓ No mistakes.

4. **I feel scared?**
   - ⓐ I feel scared!
   - ⓑ I feel scared.
   - ⓒ I feel scared,
   - ⓓ No mistakes.

5. **Jimmy's dad**
   - ⓐ Jimmy's dad sells
   - ⓑ Jimmy's dad sells computers.
   - ⓒ Jimmy's dad.
   - ⓓ No mistakes

6. **She has a tiny, small kitten.**
   - ⓐ She has a tiny kitten.
   - ⓑ She has a tiny, small, little kitten.
   - ⓒ She has a tiny, small, little, baby kitten.
   - ⓓ No mistakes.

Assessment *(cont.)*

7. **Jon likes fast cars he likes boats, too.**
   a. Jon likes fast cars! He likes boats, too.
   b. Jon likes fast cars? He likes boats, too.
   c. Jon likes fast cars. He likes boats, too.
   d. No mistakes.

8. **Dear Teacher, How are you**
   a. Dear Teacher, How are you?
   b. Dear Teacher. How are you?
   c. Dear Teacher, How are you!
   d. No mistakes.

9. **Mrs Macdonald does not like animals**
   a. Mrs. Macdonald does not like animals.
   b. Mrs Macdonald does not like animals.
   c. Mrs. Macdonald does not like animals
   d. No mistakes

10. **Where do you live?**
    a. Where do you live!
    b. Where do you live.
    c. Where do you live
    d. No mistakes.

11. **played hopscotch**
    a. played hopscotch and marbles.
    b. and played hopscotch?
    c. We played hopscotch.
    d. No mistakes.

12. **Run away from that burning building!**
    a. Run away from that burning building?
    b. Run away from that burning building.
    c. Run away from that burning building,
    d. No mistakes.

Assessment *(cont.)*

13. **She yelled and shouted for her brother.**
    ⓐ She yelled, shouted, and screamed for her brother.
    ⓑ She yelled for her brother.
    ⓒ She yelled for her brother, and shouted.
    ⓓ No mistakes.

14. **Are you invited!**
    ⓐ Are you invited.
    ⓑ Are you invited,
    ⓒ Are you invited?
    ⓓ No mistakes.

15. **My friend Tony**
    ⓐ My friend Tony Smith
    ⓑ My friend Tony saw
    ⓒ My friend Tony saw a hawk.
    ⓓ No mistakes.

16. **We ate cake then we ate ice cream.**
    ⓐ We ate cake then we ate ice cream?
    ⓑ We ate cake. Then we ate ice cream.
    ⓒ We ate cake then we ate ice cream!
    ⓓ No mistakes.

17. **Where are you going.**
    ⓐ Where are you going?
    ⓑ Where are you going,
    ⓒ Where are you going!
    ⓓ No mistakes.

18. **Dear Mom, I love you.**
    ⓐ Dear Mom. I love you.
    ⓑ Dear Mom! I love you?
    ⓒ Dear Mom I love you.
    ⓓ No mistakes.

19. The huge giant dinosaur ran after the bird.

ⓐ The huge giant dinosaur ran after the bird

ⓑ The huge, giant dinosaur ran after the bird.

ⓒ The huge dinosaur ran after the bird.

ⓓ No mistakes.

20. The skateboard is red

ⓐ The skateboard is red,

ⓑ The skateboard is red!

ⓒ The skateboard is red.

ⓓ No mistakes

21. singing a song.

ⓐ singing a song?

ⓑ Sally was singing a song.

ⓒ is singing a song.

ⓓ No mistakes.

22. I'm telling the truth.

ⓐ I'm telling the real truth.

ⓑ I'm telling the honest truth.

ⓒ I'm telling the real, honest truth.

ⓓ No mistakes.

23. aunt marge plays hockey.

ⓐ Aunt marge plays hockey.

ⓑ Aunt Marge plays hockey.

ⓒ aunt Marge plays hockey.

ⓓ No mistakes.

24. Clean your room sweep the floor.

ⓐ Clean your room. Sweep the floor.

ⓑ Clean your room! Sweep the floor?

ⓒ Clean your room sweep the floor!

ⓓ No mistakes.

25. Meg, Jim, and Katie dance at lunch.

   (a) Meg Jim and Katie dance at lunch.

   (b) Meg Jim, and Katie dance at lunch.

   (c) Meg, Jim, and Katie, dance at lunch.

   (d) No mistakes.

26. mr jones lives on main street.

   (a) Mr. Jones lives on main street.

   (b) Mr. Jones lives on Main Street.

   (c) mr. Jones lives on Main street.

   (d) No mistakes.

27. How old is your sister!

   (a) How old is your sister?

   (b) How old is your sister

   (c) How old is your sister.

   (d) No mistakes.

28. Put that fire out!

   (a) put that fire out!

   (b) Put that fire out?

   (c) Put that fire out,

   (d) No mistakes.

29. Miss Gomez is a pretty, beautiful girl.

   (a) Miss Gomez is a beautiful girl.

   (b) miss gomez is a beautiful girl.

   (c) Miss Gomez is a pretty. beautiful girl.

   (d) No mistakes.

30. The mailman likes rain he likes snow, too.

   (a) The mailman likes rain He likes snow, too.

   (b) The mailman likes rain, He likes snow, too.

   (c) The mailman likes rain. He likes snow, too.

   (d) No mistakes.

Answer Key

Page 12
1. cooked
2. baked
3. ate
4. played
5. clapped
6. sang
7. washed
8. eat

Page 15
1. was
2. am
3. are
4. looked
5. seemed
6. felt
7. were

Page 16
1. Subject: Jim and John
   Predicate: play kickball on the field.
2. Subject: The computer
   Predicate: is making funny noises.
3. Subject: Katie's hamster
   Predicate: loves carrots.
4. Subject: The crow
   Predicate: stole the farmer's corn
5. Subject: you
   Predicate: like to ride your bike in the rain.

Page 18
1. Adjective: yellow; describes *daisies*
2. Adjective: heavy; describes *box*
3. Adjective: red; describes *leaves*
4. Adjective: tall; describes *Aunt Ginny*
5. Adjectives: big and bright; describes *moon*

Page 20
1. Adverb: quickly; describes *snapped*
2. Adverb: beautifully; describes *sings*
3. Adverb: gently; describes *spoke*
4. Adverb: crazily; describes *shook*
5. Adverb: warmly; describes *shook*

Page 21
The following words should be circled:

2. walked
3. swims
4. runs
5. did
6. talked
7. cracked
8. dress

Page 22
1. Last week, Julie broke her leg.
2. Mr. Harris lives in Kentucky.
3. Do you like to watch Bugs Bunny on T.V.?
4. Suzie told Mom she wanted to go to Canada.
5. Dr. Roberts lives in the United States.

Page 23
colored blue—Mrs. Marie, Ohio, Uncle Joseph, Dr. Ruiz, Aunt Cynthia, England

colored red—truck, apple, cup, city, teacher, bird

Page 24
1. Ms. Bee ran for the bus.
2. The snake bit Dr. John on his toe.
3. I like to eat ice cream.
4. Both Jose Jr. and Mr. Sam love boats.
5. Ask Dr. Brown if you can have a lollipop.

Page 25
1. Dear Cathy, Thank you for the gift.
2. We like to run, hike, and ski.
3. Dear Sam, I like you.
4. Do you want milk, juice, or water?
5. My friends are named Charlie, Liz, and Kitty.

Page 26
1. Mrs. Jones walked a mile.
2. She went to the library, the store, and the park.
3. Dr. Katt fed ducks at the park.
4. Children threw bread, crackers, and cookies for the ducks.
5. Ralph, John, and Jenny played on the swings.
6. Mr. Jones brought his wife a letter.
7. It said, "Dear Mrs. Jones, Please call me."
8. You left your book at the store.

Page 27
Add a question mark at the end of every sentence on this page.

Answer Key (cont.)

Page 28

1. Wow! This is a fun party.
2. Hurry up and clean your room!
3. I am so angry!
4. Look out for the shark!
5. Help! Call the police!

Page 29

1. Are you afraid of spiders?
2. I am so scared!
3. Who likes insects?
4. Where can you find worms?
5. Hurry and run from that bee!
6. Which bug is your favorite?
7. Watch out for the hornet!
8. How do you catch a firefly?

Page 30

1. Student adds verb.
2. Student adds subject.
3. Student adds verb.
4. Student adds subject.
5. Student adds verb.

Page 31

1. Aunt Mary likes soap operas.
2. The baby rabbit eats lettuce.
3. That old car got a flat tire.
4. My dad wears purple neckties.
5. The cafeteria smells like cookies.

Page 32

1. Deanne drank milk. Her sister drank soda.
2. The horse ran. Then he jumped over the stream.
3. Peter loves cookies. He eats them all day.
4. I lost my lunchbox. I lost my pencil, too.
5. Ducks quack. Cows moo.

Page 33

1. The girls played soccer. They love that game.
2. Cynthia wants shoes for her birthday. She wants shorts, too.
3. The girls watch soccer on television. They cheer loudly.
4. Kick the ball. Now, run!
5. The field is damp. The girls slide on the grass.
6. They went out for pizza. They also had a slumber party.

Page 34

1. Cross out "nice."
2. Cross out "gigantic."
3. Cross out "true."
4. Cross out "small."
5. Cross out "and quiet."

Page 35

John was short. He wanted to be a tall boy. He hung upside down from a tree. That was a failure. He walked on his toes. His feet hurt. Finally, John yelled for his brothers. Paul pulled his legs. Kevin pulled his head. John yelled, "Stop!" His face was red. He decided he liked being short, after all.

Page 37

The following corrections should be made:

1. lowercase "Animals"
2. add a period after "dolphins"
3. "peeple" should be spelled "people"
4. "I also like chimpanzees" should start a new paragraph
5. "cecil" should be capitalized
6. comma after "plants"
7. comma after "meat"
8. period after "insects"
9. "eeting" should be spelled "eating"

Page 42–46

1. C	7. C	13. B	19. C	25. D
2. B	8. A	14. C	20. C	26. B
3. D	9. A	15. C	21. B	27. A
4. A	10. D	16. B	22. D	28. D
5. B	11. C	17. A	23. B	29. A
6. A	12. D	18. D	24. A	30. C